W9-APS-185

TONY STEWART

Jeff Burton

Dale Earnhardt Jr.

Famous Finishes

Famous Tracks

Kenny Irwin Jr.

Jimmie Johnson

The Labonte Brothers

Lowriders

Monster Trucks & Tractors

Motorcycles

Off-Road Racing

Rockcrawling

Tony Stewart

The Unsers

Rusty Wallace

TONY STEWART

Tara Baukus Mello

CHELSEA HOUSE
PUBLISHERS
A Haights Cross Communications Company ®
Philadelphia

Cover Photo: NASCAR driver Tony Stewart is shown watching the qualifying runs at Bristol Motor Speedway in Bristol, Tennessee on April 1, 2005.

CHELSEA HOUSE PUBLISHERS

VP, NEW PRODUCT DEVELOPMENT   Sally Cheney
DIRECTOR OF PRODUCTION   Kim Shinners
CREATIVE MANAGER   Takeshi Takahashi
MANUFACTURING MANAGER   Diann Grasse

STAFF FOR TONY STEWART

EDITORIAL ASSISTANT Sarah Sharpless
PRODUCTION EDITOR Bonnie Cohen
PHOTO EDITOR Pat Holl
SERIES DESIGN AND LAYOUT Hierophant Publishing Services/EON PreMedia

Original edition first published in 2001.

http://www.chelseahouse.com

A Haights Cross Communications ◤ Company ®

First Printing

1   3   5   7   9   8   6   4   2

Library of Congress Cataloging-in-Publication Data

Mello, Tara Baukus.
   Tony Stewart / Tara Baukus Mello.
      p. cm.—(Race car legends. Collector's edition)
   ISBN 0-7910-8670-4
  1. Stewart, Tony, 1971—Juvenile literature. 2. Stock car drivers–United States–Biograhy–Juvenile literature. 3. NASCAR (Association)–Juvenile literature. I. Title. II. Series.
GV1032.S743M45 2 005
796.72'092–dc22

                                        2005010505

TABLE OF CONTENTS

① WINNING ROOKIE

Only two races were left in the 1999 NASCAR Winston Cup season (now known as the Nextel Cup) when Tony Stewart and his fellow drivers headed to the Homestead-Miami Speedway in South Florida. Tony and the Home Depot team were in fourth place for the year, a remarkable spot for a rookie, a driver in his first season of racing. At age 28, Tony had definitely caught the attention of veteran drivers like Mark Martin and Dale Jarrett. Everyone seemed to agree that Tony was already a contender on the racetrack—no small feat for a rookie.

The last rookie to get this much attention in Cup racing was Jeff Gordon, when he entered the circuit in 1993. Jeff is a remarkable driver, who won three NASCAR Cup championships before he turned 27. However, Jeff had not shown nearly as much promise in his rookie year as Tony did in his first season. In 1999, Tony finished in fifth place or higher 12 times, breaking the record for a rookie year, previously held by Dale Earnhardt Sr. in 1979.

After driving well throughout the 1999 season, Tony marked September by winning the Exide NASCAR Select Batteries 400. The win made him the first rookie to win a NASCAR race since the late Davey Allison in 1987. A few

A pace car (left) leads drivers during the start of the Pennzoil 400 in the NASCAR Cup Series on November 14, 1999, at Homestead-Miami Speedway in Homestead, Florida. It was the first Cup event held at the track, and Tony Stewart won by 5.289 seconds.

months later, Tony tied Davey's record of two wins in a rookie season by being first at the Checker Auto Parts/Dura Lube 500. Winning two races in his first season was an amazing accomplishment. It was so unusual that everyone seemed to expect that Tony would finish the last two races of the season holding his own on the track. But they didn't expect him to win again. No rookie had ever won three races in the entire 52-year history of NASCAR racing.

The Pennzoil 400, presented by Kmart, was the first Cup Series race to be held at the Homestead-Miami Speedway. In

1995, the track opened to both Busch and Craftsman Truck Series racing, two other racing series overseen by NASCAR (National Association for Stock Car Auto Racing). More than 300,000 fans came each year to the 1.5-mile oval to watch their favorite drivers compete. Many more fans were expected to visit the Florida track for its first Cup race in 1999.

For many drivers, the Pennzoil 400 was an important race to win. Because it was the first Cup race to be held at this track, drivers were eager to add the win to their record. Veteran driver Dale Jarrett would have especially liked to win the race because he had won the first Busch Series race held at the Homestead-Miami Speedway. Dale was also in the lead for the championship. He was ahead by enough points that he only needed to finish in eighth place or higher to win the 1999 championship. It didn't seem likely, however, that Dale would win the race; the Pontiacs seemed to be the strongest competitors on the track during the Friday qualifying meets, taking six of the top seven starting positions.

David Green of Tyler Jet Motorsports had won the pole position, meaning that he would start the race in first place. It was the first time David had gained the pole position in a Cup race. Winning was very important to David because he wasn't sure he'd have a sponsor to race for in the next season. He also knew that some people were questioning his ability as a driver.

Tony was at the top of the list of Pontiac drivers favored to win the race and started in seventh place. Jeff Gordon said that Tony was pretty fast on the track: "I was just hoping and praying I could stay within sight of him. They're [the Home Depot team] pretty awesome."

Bobby Labonte, Tony's teammate at Joe Gibbs Racing, was also a favorite to win, starting third.

Tony Stewart's pit crew demonstrates speed and precision during a pit stop at the 1999 Pennzoil 400. The crew's ability to get Tony in and out of the pit quickly was critical to Tony's victory in the race.

The Homestead-Miami Speedway is different from other 1.5-mile tracks where Cup races are held. This track has long, flat corners, which means that they seem even longer than they actually are. Because of the design of the track, it is difficult for drivers to race side by side, which is one of the things that makes a Cup race exciting. Dale Jarrett explained, "You have to work hard to get your car to handle through the corners. Obviously, getting off the corners is very important to be able to utilize the straightaway."

When the Pennzoil 400 began, Bobby Labonte took the lead from Green on lap 27. Bobby's driving was strong, and he led the race four times for the first 174 laps. Tony worked his way into the lead for the first time on lap 123, but held the top position for only two laps. On lap 187, competitor Ricky Rudd blew his engine, and a caution flag—the only one in the race—came out. When Bobby decided to use the caution to come in for a pit stop, Tony took the lead again. Their two Pontiacs continued to battle, trading the lead back and forth. It turned out that the last time the drivers came in for their pit stops would be critical to the race.

At lap 244 of the 400-mile race, Bobby realized that he wouldn't be able to finish without stopping for fuel one last time. He pulled in for his final pit stop, spending 8.7 seconds getting fuel and two new tires for the right side. The team believed the new tires might give Bobby the boost he needed to regain the lead and keep it, winning the race. A few laps later, Tony also stopped in the pits for fuel and two new tires. His team worked a bit faster, completing the pit stop in just 8.0 seconds, giving Tony a little bit of an advantage when he reentered the track.

When Tony drove out of pit lane and back onto the track, he ended up right next to Bobby. Tony's spotter, a team member who watches the race from high up and acts as a second set of eyes for his driver, told Tony what was about to happen. Tony tried to enter the track just in front of Bobby by accelerating as fast as he could. Instead, the two ended up racing side by side between Turns 2 and 3. As the pair entered Turn 3, Tony's car, which was on the inside of the track near the infield, lost traction. He bumped into his teammate, causing Bobby to fall several positions behind.

Tony told reporters after the race that he didn't mean to bump into his teammate. He explained,

> He did what he had to do, and I did what I had to do. We're both here to win. I couldn't stay that far down on the apron and the car got loose and I wiggled up the racetrack and got into him. It wasn't anything intentional.

The bump meant that Bobby, who was in second place for the championship behind Dale Jarrett, lost his chance at passing Dale in points and winning the championship. Still, Bobby accepted Tony's apology, saying, "I don't think it mattered. I wouldn't have beat him anyway. I couldn't figure out my tires today. That was my fault."

On lap 258, Tony took the lead for the last time when Mark Martin went in for his final pit stop. After leading four times for a total of 43 laps, Tony won the race by 5.289 seconds, almost an entire straightaway. His win, the third in his first year of Cup racing, meant that he had more wins than any other rookie driver in the history of the sport. Not only was Tony going to win NASCAR's Rookie of the Year award but he was also the best rookie driver anyone had ever seen.

"It's a great honor to be a part of the series this year and be associated with Joe Gibbs Racing and Home Depot . . . .

DID YOU KNOW?

Pit crews rehearse their pit stops several times a week in an effort to move as quickly as they can. All members are also required to lift weights twice a week to help them stay in shape. Although the pit crew spends more time waiting during the race than actually performing pit stops, being a member of the pit crew is very hard work. Once the driver pulls into the pits, crew members must spring into action as quickly as they can, often carrying heavy items, such as a 90-pound gas can over a foot-high wall.

Performing a good pit stop can be a challenge. Every member of the crew has to be precise for things to go smoothly. Even then, if another team is faster, it can mean the difference between winning and losing. "When you're in school, a 95 percent will get you an A," said Charles "Ronny" Crooks, a former member of Tony's pit crew. "Here, a 95 will get you a D or an F. You need to be perfect."

Tony Stewart has a lot to smile about in Victory Lane after the Pennzoil 400, his third win of 1999. That year, he set a new record for most wins by a rookie driver in the Cup Series.

Bobby [Labonte] really helped me get into that second car. It's just a great honor to be associated with them," commented Tony.

Tony's rookie year was stunning. It had been 41 years since NASCAR started the Rookie of the Year award, and during that time only seven rookies had finished in the top 10 for the season. Of those seven drivers, only one, James Hylton, did better than Tony's fourth-place finish, but that

Dale Jarrett (center) poses with his family after winning the 1999 NASCAR Cup Series championship at the Homestead-Miami Speedway. Jarrett finished fifth in the Pennzoil 400 to clinch the honor.

was in 1966, more than 30 years earlier. Even three-time Cup champion Jeff Gordon only placed 14th in his rookie season.

Not only were Tony's standings at the end of the season impressive but his driving throughout the year was also incredible. He led more laps than any other driver during the second half of the season and was second with 1,223 laps for the entire year. He led just 97 laps fewer than lap leader Jeff Gordon for the 1999 season.

Although Tony's achievement was tremendous, he still had to share the spotlight. Dale Jarrett, the leader in the Cup

Series, finished the Pennzoil 400 in fifth place and received enough points to win the Cup Championship. It was Dale's first championship, and with it he won the distinction of becoming one of only two father-son duos to win NASCAR Championship titles. His father, Ned Jarrett, won two series championships, and Lee and Richard Petty also won NASCAR Championship titles.

Dale drove solidly throughout the race, staying in the top 10 for the entire 400 miles. "He did exactly what he had to do, and he did it with class," said Tony of Dale. "He's a great person. You can learn a lot from somebody like that."

2

EARLY YEARS

Tony was just eight years old when he started racing. It was 1979 and Tony had been "driving" in a child-sized car in the backyard of his home. His mom came out of the house and saw that her son had torn up the grass with the car. She recognized Tony's early passion for cars and got him started in go-karts. Tony's interest in racing developed quickly, and soon he was spending his weekends and time after school at racetracks.

Tony Stewart was born in Columbus, Indiana, on May 20, 1971, and lived there with his parents and younger sister, Natalie, until he graduated from high school. When he was 18, he moved to Rushville, Indiana, to advance his racing career. Like the residents of Columbus, the people of Rushville also became big fans of his. Today, Tony calls both cities his hometowns. And the communities were so proud of him that both mayors gave him the keys to their cities. As Tony's career progressed, racing became his whole life. Tony regularly chose racing over spending time with his friends.

Today, Tony is a very private person. While he is appreciative of his fans, he wants them to respect his privacy. As a result, he doesn't talk about his personal life and doesn't usually sign autographs for fans, except at organized autograph

Tony Stewart signs autographs for fans on pit road prior to qualifying for a NASCAR Busch Series race. While Tony appreciates his fans, he doesn't talk about his personal life and he likes fans to respect his privacy.

sessions. Too often fans have swarmed around him, seeking autographs and photos as he left the garage or the racetrack. Once he was hit in the shoulder with a helmet falling from a fan who was pushed into him. Another time, one of Tony's friends was nearly knocked to the ground by fans trying to get to him while he was at the track.

"I feel like I'm in jail," Tony said. "I've got to be either in my room or in this trailer or in my garage. Those are the only three places I can have time to myself." Many of the most popular NASCAR drivers are in similar situations, but it wasn't always that way for Tony. Early in his career, it was a struggle just to be able to have enough money to keep racing.

Auto racing is an expensive sport, which is why professional racers have multimillion-dollar sponsorships with large companies, as Tony does with The Home Depot. But in amateur racing, many competitors get only smaller sponsors who give just small amounts of money or parts in exchange for having their business's name displayed on the side of the car. Sometimes amateur racers don't have sponsors at all. In Tony's early days of racing, his parents mortgaged their house to make sure that they had enough money to keep Tony racing.

He first competed in go-karts and then, when he was in high school, he began racing three-quarter midgets, open-wheel cars that are most often raced on dirt tracks. At age 21, Tony began racing full-time in the United States Auto Club (USAC) league, which includes three different series—Silver Crown, Sprint, and Midget cars. USAC races are run on oval tracks with a dirt surface, and all the cars have exposed wheels. Silver Crown cars race on both dirt and oval tracks. USAC racing is usually a lot of fun to watch because the cars often slide around the corners, almost as if they were out of control. Sometimes the cars do lose control and roll sideways multiple times, creating spectacular accidents. Despite these serious accidents, drivers usually are not hurt because of heavy-duty roll cages, steel bars that surround the driver and protect his body.

When Tony was in the USAC league, he raced all over the Midwest, frequently driving from one state to another to compete in several races during the same weekend. In addition to competing in several races over a few days, Tony also often drove different cars. For example, on a weekend in August 1995, he first competed in both a Midget race and a Silver Crown race in Springfield, Illinois. Then he drove

Tony Stewart began racing full-time in the USAC at the age of 21, competing in Silver Crown, Midget, and Sprint cars. Spectacular accidents like the Sprint cars shown here make USAC races fun to watch. The drivers are protected by a heavy-duty roll cage.

to another Midget race in Granite City, Illinois, on Saturday night, followed by a Sprint car race in Salem, Indiana on Sunday.

Tony described the switch from Midget cars to Silver Crown cars as "going from a Chevette to a Cadillac." He explained, "You drive both of them just as hard, but when you do something with the steering wheel or the throttle, it happens quicker with the Midget."

After a few years of racing open-wheel cars, Tony was well known in the league. In 1994, he won USAC's National Midget championship. The following year, Tony was aiming for an even bigger title. The three different types of USAC racing—Sprint, Midget, and Silver Crown—each had its own championship title. A driver who wins all three championships once is said to have won the "Triple Crown" in USAC racing. Although a few other drivers had won the Triple Crown, no racer had ever won all three championships in the same year. Tony was hoping to be the first driver to win this important title.

"I set goals to make me push myself," he said during the middle of that race season. "[Winning the Triple Crown] was our goal when we started the season, and I think it's realistic." Tony was right—he hadn't set his goals too high. He raced well all season long and, in the end, became the first—and so far, the only—person to win the USAC Triple Crown in the same year.

Winning all three championships in 1995 meant that Tony's name became even more well-known than before. Many people considered him to be the hottest young racer they had seen in a long time. Some thought that he had the potential to succeed in any type of racing. Tony's success meant he had to make a choice before he moved up to the next level. He had to choose between NASCAR stock cars and Indy cars. Tony grew up in Indiana, where the most popular race in the entire state is the Indianapolis 500. Like many kids who were interested in racing, it was Tony's dream to win the Indy 500 someday. So when it came time to choose, Tony opted first for Indy car racing in the Indy Racing League (IRL).

The Indianapolis Motor Speedway is the home of the Indy 500. Like many boys growing up in Indiana, Tony Stewart dreamed of someday winning that famous race.

The IRL was formed in 1995, and it held only three races in 1996. That meant Tony had a lot of free time that year, which he, of course, spent racing in other series. He continued to race Sprints, Midgets, and Silver Crown cars for USAC and also competed in nine races in the NASCAR Busch Series.

"When I was growing up, I never decided I wanted to drive just stock cars or just drive Indy cars. Whatever was on TV that day, by gosh, that's what I wanted to drive," Tony admitted.

Tony's driving skills on dirt tracks came in handy when he competed in Indy racing. During his first IRL race, which was also the first IRL race ever, Tony finished second after some pretty unusual driving. A bad crash occurred on lap 185 during the Indy 200, which was held on a new track at Walt Disney World in Orlando, Florida. Cars went spinning all over the track, and when Tony came upon the wreck a safety vehicle blocked his path. Tony used a Sprint-car style technique—driving left, right, and then left—to get around the crash. During the driving maneuver, Tony scraped the wall with his right-side wheels, and he was forced to drive over debris left on the track from the cars that had crashed.

Even Tony was surprised that he had escaped without harm to his car. "I hit the wall pretty hard and I ran over a lot of debris. I was afraid all four tires were going to have a cut in them, let alone a bent race car," he recalled.

Good driving mixed with a little bit of luck is what put Tony on the pole in the Indianapolis 500 later that year. In practice at the Indy 500, Tony drove a 237-miles-per-hour lap—the fastest lap next to veteran driver Arie Luyendyk. During qualifying, Tony had the third-fastest speed. Arie logged the top speed, 236.986 miles per hour, while the second qualifier was Tony's teammate, Scott Brayton.

Did you know?

A Silver Crown car looks similar to a Sprint car, but is larger. Silver Crown are powered by big engines that typically produce more than 700 horsepower and can propel the car to speeds of up to 170 miles per hour on the straight section, called a straightaway, at an oval track. Silver Crown races are longer than Sprint or Midget races, usually 100 miles or 100 laps around the track.

During practice for the 1998 Indy 500, Tony Stewart gets some advice from team manager Larry Curry (left) and chief mechanic Bill Martin (right).

But two unique events put Tony on the pole. First, race organizers had determined that Arie's car was seven pounds underweight. Because of this fact, Arie's first qualifying run wasn't allowed, and he lost his chance at the pole. Then, after qualifying in first place, Scott Brayton was killed in a crash during practice. These two events left Tony to start first in the Indy 500, making him the youngest driver to be on the pole in 50 years.

Despite the terrible tragedy, the team decided to move forward and compete in the race.

"I hope no one judges us today as coming out and running as being callous, like we don't care," said Larry Curry, the team manager. "We certainly care. But the point is, if Scott was here, he would be the first one to be telling me, 'Hey, how are you guys going to learn anything sitting in the garage?'"

From 1996 until 1999, Tony continued to race in many different series, including the NASCAR Busch Series, which led him to his full-time career in NASCAR Cup racing. In 1998, he raced in the IRL full-time and competed in another 22 races in the Busch Series for Joe Gibbs's racing team. Many people view NASCAR's Busch Series as one that helps prepare many young and inexperienced drivers for the Cup circuit. Although the stock cars used in the Busch Series are quite similar to Cup cars, there are also many very important differences.

NASCAR Cup cars are significantly longer and much heavier than those used in the Busch Series. In addition, the Cup cars produce as much as 200 more horsepower than Busch cars do.

"I think the Busch Series is a pretty good training ground," longtime NASCAR Cup driver Rusty Wallace said. "But I can tell you that when I drove a NASCAR truck once at Nazareth [Pennsylvania], it was a lot closer to a Winston Cup car than a Busch car."

Although Tony's next step was into a NASCAR Cup car, it really didn't matter to him whether or not the Busch Series was good training. For Tony, racing was his hobby as well as his job, so he competed as often as he could, in whatever cars he could. It remains that way to this day.

"I learn something every day that I get in a race car," Tony said. "People think I'm racing just to race. Well, that's my hobby, too. Getting in a Midget or getting in my dirt late model or some of these other cars that I run, that's my release, how I get away from the IRL series and the NASCAR series."

TWO RACES, SAME DAY

Imagine taking a trip from New York City to Orlando, Florida, in just one day, not stopping to eat or to use the bathroom. Then imagine taking the trip in the summer in a car with no air conditioning, while wearing long underwear and a heavy winter coat. Imagine one of your parents driving on this trip, concentrating really hard because lots of cars on the road are zigzagging all around your car. If you can imagine all of this, then you would have an idea of what it was like for Tony to drive more than 1,000 miles in two races on the same day.

On May 30, 1999, Tony made history by competing in the Indy 500 in Indianapolis, Indiana, and then the Coca-Cola 600, the longest race on the NASCAR Cup circuit, in Charlotte, North Carolina. Only one driver, John Andretti, had ever tried it before, and he crashed before the end of the Coca-Cola 600. Tony not only completed the two races but also finished in the Top 10 in both.

The fact that Tony was going to compete in another league when he was already racing full-time on the NASCAR Cup circuit was very unusual, but it was something he really wanted to do. It was Tony's dream to win the Indianapolis 500, and he was determined to keep trying even though he was already committed to another racing league.

May 30, 1999, was a historic day for Tony Stewart. He raced in both the Indianapolis 500 (shown here) and the Coca-Cola 600, which is hundreds of miles away from Indianapolis in North Carolina.

Tony explained, "I grew up in Columbus, Indiana, and every May you're still in school and the only thing you want to do is get home and watch the 5 and 6 o'clock news to see who is running fast [at the Indianapolis Motor Speedway]. I'm a young race driver from Indiana, and I'd be stupid if I didn't say this was the single most important race to me."

Competing in two races in the same day took a lot of planning. Because of the timing of the two races and the amount of time it takes to fly from Indianapolis to Charlotte, Tony's entire day was planned down to the minute. The team had done as much preparation as they could, but there was still one thing that no one could control—the weather. If conditions were bad in Indianapolis and the race started late, then it might not be over by the time Tony needed to leave for the race in Charlotte.

"My number one priority is the Winston Cup program," Tony said. "If we were leading Indy with five laps to go and it was time to go on the airplane, I would have to leave."

When Tony woke up in his motor home on the infield at the Indianapolis Motor Speedway at 9:30 A.M. on Sunday, May 30, the weather was good. His crew had already been working for more than five hours preparing his car.

Tony started 24th in Indy 500 and began passing other cars, even though his car wasn't handling as well as he had hoped. At each pit stop the team made adjustments, and Tony kept passing other drivers and increasing his chances of winning. But in a pit stop near the end of the race, the crew had trouble with the jack, and Tony ended up running over it and damaging the car slightly. The damage meant that he lost his chance at winning the race. When the Indy 500 concluded at 3:15 P.M., Tony was in ninth place. Even with the problems, it was Tony's second-best finish ever for the Indy 500.

Tony was scheduled to start 27th at the Coca-Cola 600 Nextel Cup race in North Carolina. To start in this position, however, he had to attend the drivers' meeting, which began at 4:15 P.M. To get to Lowe's Motor Speedway as quickly as possible, Tony took a golf cart, two helicopters, and a private jet. Despite this great effort, he still missed the drivers' meeting and had to start last. This meant that instead of starting 27th, Tony would be the 43rd car to take off from the starting line.

Within the first 10 laps of the race, Tony had moved up to 33rd place. On lap 80, Tony told his crew he wasn't feeling very well. With all the time spent racing, he hadn't eaten much all day. It was starting to get to him, but Tony pressed

Tony Stewart (second from the right) is taken to his race car for the start of the Coca-Cola 600 after arriving at the track by helicopter. At the end of the day Tony was exhausted, but he finished in the top five—an amazing display of determination and endurance.

on. At lap 100, about an hour after the race started, Tony was in eighth place. A short time later, Tony battled his team-mate, Bobby Labonte, and took the lead. Tony continued to race up front, trading the lead with Bobby, Mark Martin, and Jeff Burton for nearly 200 laps. With just 80 laps left in the 400-lap race, Tony began to feel very sick and dizzy. He kept racing, but it was a struggle. Cars began to pass him.

"I never use the head rest in cars, and I used the head rest the last 60–70 laps," he said. "I felt like I was about 90 percent and leaving 10 percent on the table. I was just trying to make sure I didn't make a mistake and could bring the car home."

In the end, Tony crossed the line fourth. After racing 1,090 miles in one day, Tony was exhausted. When he

Tony Stewart streaks down the front stretch at Lowe's Motor Speedway during the 1999 Coca-Cola 600. By the end of that day, he had driven 1,090 miles in two races.

climbed out of his car, his legs buckled, and he sank to the ground. A medical crew took him on a stretcher to the track hospital. When Tony was released, he wearily told the press that he was ready for a nap. "I should have planned better," Tony said. "We were so concerned with keeping fluid in me, we didn't think about getting food in."

When it was over, Tony said he couldn't imagine competing in both races on the same day again. Much to everyone's surprise, two years later he decided that he wanted to try it again. "The only reason I did it this year again was because I thought it was the right opportunity with the right team to do it," explained Tony when he announced his plan to compete in both races again in 2001.

Just like his first attempt at what he called "Double Duty," every moment of Tony's day was planned down to the last detail: how long the Indy 500 lasted, what to do if there were weather issues, and how Tony was feeling. Joe Gibbs, the owner of Tony's NASCAR team, said,

"We think that this is a good opportunity for him and Home Depot to achieve this dream. In the case of any conflicts, Tony's number one responsibility will be the #20 Home Depot car and the Coca-Cola 600. We have made all arrangements to assure that Tony will start the Coca-Cola 600."

On May 28, 2001, at noon, the green flag fell and the 85th running of the Indianapolis 500 began. Tony started in seventh place and then dropped to 10th place. After several pit stops in the first 80 laps to make adjustments to the car, Tony again started to work his way through the pack. He was in fourth place when a caution flag brought the leading cars in for a quick pit stop, giving Tony the opportunity to take the lead.

Tony was the first one out of the pits. As he was driving down pit road, two of the other race leaders, teammates Gil de Ferran and Helio Castroneves, pulled out in front of Tony. Tony hit the brakes, but John Andretti, who was behind Tony, was unable to stop in time. He bumped into Tony but only caused damage to his own car.

The IRL officials who were watching the race decided that what Gil and Helio did was against the rules, and they awarded the lead spot to Tony. He held the lead for 12 laps. By lap 150, Tony began to get a cramp in his right leg. At the same time, a rainstorm was threatening the race and, five laps later, IRL officials temporarily stopped the race due to the rain.

Because his car was parked, Tony decided he would visit the drivers' first aid center and try to get some help for his leg cramp. Therapists had only a few minutes to massage his right hamstring muscle before the sun came out and the announcement was made for the drivers to get back into their cars. When Tony heard the announcement, he left the first aid station and hopped into a golf cart to get back to his car quickly. The golf-cart driver had misunderstood, however, and thought that it was too late and Tony needed to leave the race and go to Charlotte for the NASCAR race. Instead of driving toward Tony's race car, the driver began to drive Tony away from the track and toward the helicopter.

Tony jumped off the golf cart and started running toward his car. He got going quickly, and when the officials restarted the race on lap 158, he was fifth. Later, during another pit stop, Tony stalled the car right as the jack dropped him back to the ground. He lost about five seconds in the pits before he could get going again. In the end, Tony crossed the finish line in fifth place and quickly took off for the Coca-Cola 600 in Charlotte, North Carolina.

The helicopter that carried Tony to the Charlotte Motor Speedway landed in the infield just in time for the drivers'

DID YOU KNOW?

Veteran racer Robby Gordon has tried to compete in both the Indianapolis 500 and the Coca-Cola 600 on the same day for four years. In three of Robby's four attempts, weather caused problems. In 2004, rain delayed the start of the Indy 500 by two hours and 11 minutes and Robby was only able to race 28 laps before he had to leave to fly to Charlotte to compete in the NASCAR race. Robby had hoped that the weather would delay the race until another day, when he could return to compete. Unfortunately, the rain let up and Robby's crew member, Jacques Lazier, took over the driving. Jacques completed only 88 laps after having to drop out of the race due to mechanical problems with the car.

introductions. Just as in the first Double Duty, Tony had to start in last place because he had missed the mandatory drivers' meeting. After a bit of a struggle and several pit stops for adjustments, Tony began to work his way through the field of drivers and was in 15th place by lap 180 and 10th place by lap 265. By lap 370 of the 400-lap race, Tony had passed Dale Jarrett and moved into fifth, then soon passed Jimmy Spencer. On lap 387, Tony was able to pass Mark Martin and move into third place. With just 13 laps left, however, that was the best Tony was able to do.

At the end of Tony's second attempt at Double Duty, he drove 1,100 miles in about eight hours, placing sixth at the Indianapolis 500 and third at the Coca-Cola 600. While his effort was a personal accomplishment, Tony also raced as a way to raise money for charity. Before the race, Tony pledged $100 for every lap he raced in both events. Tony's sponsor, The Home Depot, the owner of Tony's NASCAR car, Target Chip Ganassi Racing, the owner of Tony's Indy Car, and, Joe Gibbs Racing, each said they would match Tony's pledge. The benefitting charity was the Victory Junction Gang Camp, a camp for sick children founded by NASCAR racer Kyle Petty and his family. Because Tony completed all 600 laps, he raised the maximum amount for the Camp—$240,000.

At the end of the Coca-Cola 600, Tony said that racing for the charity, "gave both of these races a purpose, rather than being something selfish that I wanted to do for my personal goals and my personal dreams. We were able to do something very productive tonight and help a lot of good kids that deserve this . . . . That is probably what I'm most proud of today."[1]

YOUNG CHAMPION

Tony's fourth year on the NASCAR Cup racing circuit, in 2002, was filled with some amazing highs and lows. At just 31 years of age, he logged his first championship, winning three races and finishing in the top five in 12 others. In the same year, however, Tony also logged six DNFs or "did-not-finish," due to accidents or car problems. On multiple occasions, Tony's temper got the best of him, and several times he was fined by NASCAR. Eventually, Tony was placed on probation.

The year got off to a rocky start when Tony was forced to leave the Daytona 500, the first points race of the Cup Series, on the second lap due to mechanical problems. It was a lousy way for Tony and The Home Depot team to start the season, but he still had high hopes for his NASCAR career that year. "Let's see what they say when we win the championship,"[2] Tony said to reporters as he left the garage that day.

By March, after logging two top-5 finishes and one win in just four races, people were starting to speculate that 2002 might be Tony's year to win the championship. Indeed, Tony had been one of the top 10 drivers in the Cup Series every year he had competed. In 2001, Tony finished second, losing the championship to Jeff Gordon by 349 points. Once again,

Tony Stewart (left) collides with Kurt Busch during the New England 300 at the New Hampshire International Speedway (NHIS) in Loudon, New Hampshire, on July 21, 2002. Tony had to drop out of the race after the incident.

however, luck was not on Tony's side and, the fifth race of the season, the Carolina Dodge Dealers 400, turned dangerous.

It looked as if Tony was headed for his second win in a row when fellow driver Buckshot Jones lost control of his car, causing Tony to run into him. The collision sent Tony's Pontiac into the outside retaining wall and then across the track, where Jimmy Spencer hit him. The force of this crash sent Tony's car spinning around and knocked him unconscious. Tony was unconscious for only about one minute, but he had to be hospitalized overnight for tests. The accident meant Tony had his second DNF of the year in only five races.

The following Sunday, Tony was back in the driver's seat for the Food City 500, but he was unable to complete the race. On lap 284, Tony began to get sore, and on lap 365, he spun the car. He decided to come into pit row and get fellow driver Todd Bodine to take over for him while the race was under a caution flag. Bodine started the race in 21st place and was able to move forward to finish 15th. At the end of the race, Bodine said,

"I got in, and I don't know if the car was getting loose and that's why Tony spun out or what, but when I got in, the car was just really, really loose. I fought it the whole time and about spun out a couple of times. If he can drive it like that, he is my hero. I can tell you that."[3]

Things did not get much better in the following few races. Tony had another DNF and then two 29th-place finishes in a row, which dropped him to 10th in the points standings. But Tony's roller-coaster ride of a year headed up again in Richmond, Virginia, at the Pontiac Excitement 400. There Tony won his second race of the season, although it was not without its challenges.

Tony qualified in third position, but rain forced NASCAR officials to postpone the race until the following day after the drivers had completed only 74 laps. That night, while the Joe Gibbs Racing crew members were performing a routine engine inspection, they discovered a problem with the engine in the car of Tony's teammate Bobby Labonte. When crew members checked Tony's car, they found the same problem. The only thing to do was to replace the engines in both cars. According to NASCAR rules, however, doing so meant that both drivers would be forced to start at the back of the pack.

After the race, Tony said, "Starting the race from the back was hard. Our car wasn't terrible, but it wasn't the way we wanted it either. With the tires as hard as they were and with the amount of sealer put down, it was a one-groove racetrack. It got to where when you were behind somebody, there was an aero push. It was the first time I've been to Richmond where aerodynamics played a part."[4]

Tony started at the back and the racing conditions were not great. But he was able to work his way through the pack of cars and into third place on lap 340, and then eventually into first place. When Tony crossed the finish line, he was almost 1.5 seconds ahead of the second-place finisher, rookie Ryan Newman.

While Tony's racing grew stronger and he logged two pole positions in the Dodge/Save-Mart 350 and the Brickyard 400, things again took a downturn. After holding the lead four times during the Brickyard 400 and looking as if he might win, Tony's hopes were dashed in the final laps. Upset that he had lost, Tony hit a newspaper photographer who was trying to take his picture after the race. NASCAR officials fined Tony $10,000 and placed him on probation for the incident. In addition, Tony's sponsor fined him another $50,000 and also placed him on probation.

Tony had lost his temper before, but this time was the worst. He decided he needed to talk to a counselor to help him learn to control his anger. Tony said,

> I know I have a problem with keeping my emotions in check. After all of this, I've felt as low as I've ever felt. But it's probably exactly what I needed to make me seek help. A hard fall like this will tend to jar you back to reality. I'm looking forward to making myself better, better as a person and better in dealing with the things life sends your way—the good and the bad.[5]

By the time the next race arrived, Tony and his team had gotten past all the emotions of the prior week and were ready to give it their all. The team and The Home Depot car were strong in practice, and Tony qualified third for the Sirius

Tony Stewart gained a reputation for not being able to control his explosive temper. He finally sought professional help after he was fined a total of $60,000 and put on probation for hitting a photographer.

Satellite Radio at Watkins Glen race. On race day, Tony led three times for a total of 34 laps in the 90-lap race.

Once, when Tony was trying to take the lead in the race, he miscalculated one of the turns and locked up his brakes, bumping into Robby Gordon's race car in the process. Explaining the bump, Tony said, "I felt bad I run into Robby . . . . I didn't mean to get into him intentionally. We

Tony Stewart celebrates in the Sirius Satellite Radio at The Glen, his third victory of the 2002 season. The win earned him enough points to put winning the Nextel Cup series championship within reach.

waved at each other on the next yellow so we both knew everything was all right."[6]

Despite several other drivers who had trouble on the race course, Tony raced strong. He was able to keep the lead twice when the race was restarted and led for the last 18 laps, winning for the third time that season. Tony's win also meant something else very important: He had earned enough points to make winning the series championship a strong possibility. Only 104 points separated him from the points leader, Sterling Marlin.

Perhaps even more importantly, the win had given Tony the opportunity to enjoy his job. He said, "This past weekend was the most fun we've had at the track in a quite a while. And look at the results."[7]

Tony's win at Watkins Glen was the last race he won that season, but he continued to race well over the next two months. In early October, after placing second in the EA Sports 500 at Talladega Superspeedway, Tony became the points leader. While Tony had been the points leader in other types of racing, this was the first time that he'd led in the NASCAR Cup series. With six races left in the season, Tony and his team knew that anything could happen. At the same time, they were hoping to win the championship.

Tony said that winning the championship "would mean more than anything."[8] He explained, "Everybody in this garage area is searching for a Winston Cup championship —even guys that have won it three or four times. Everybody wants to keep winning Winston Cup championships. That's what we're all striving for."[9]

Although the points race was tight for the final six races, Tony was able to remain in the lead the entire time. On November 17, 2002, Tony won his first NASCAR Cup Series championship. It was Tony's sixth championship in a major racing series in only eight years and the ninth championship win of his career.

Tony had gone into the Ford 400, the final race of the season, hoping to win. But his crew could not find the right setup for Tony's car to make it competitive. Instead, Tony found himself dodging accidents in front of him just after two of the race's restarts. The first close call came on lap 236 when John Andretti's engine blew. Tony was right behind John when it happened and had to think quickly and drive low on the track's apron in order to avoid hitting John's car. When the race was restarted after the accident was cleared,

Did you know?

The NASCAR Cup Series championship is given to the driver who has the most points at the end of the season, not to the driver who wins the most races. The race winner receives 180 points, while the runner-up receives 170 points. The number of points a driver is awarded drops from there in either three-, four- or five-point increments, depending on where the driver finished. The last place driver gets 34 points. All drivers get an extra five points for every lap they lead, and the driver who leads the most laps gets an additional five points.

After the 26th race of the season, the Top 10 drivers and any other drivers within 400 points of the leader are placed in the "Chase for the Championship." The drivers placed in this group have their point totals adjusted. The first-place driver is awarded 5,050 points, and the rest of the drivers in the "chase" are ranked with just five points between them. For example, the second-place driver gets 5,045 points, while the driver in third gets 5,040 points, and so on. These drivers then begin collecting points again for the remainder of the races.

Champion racer Tony Stewart poses with the Championship Trophy at the NASCAR Nextel Cup Series Awards on December 6, 2002.

Tony had another close call. He was driving next to Jason Leffler when Ricky Rudd tried to pass Jason low on the track. The three cars were caught driving side-by-side through two turns, with Tony closest to the wall.

If Tony had crashed during either close call or had a problem with his car during the race, he could have lost the championship to fellow driver Mark Martin, who was just 89 points behind Tony. Instead, Tony did everything he could to stay out of trouble and finished 18th in the race. While it was far from one of his best races of the year, it didn't matter. It was enough to give him the championship title.

After winning the championship Tony wrote about his experience for the book *Chicken Soup for the NASCAR Soul*. He wrote,

> As I think about this last season, and how our Home Depot team rebounded from a disastrous start at Daytona . . . I still have a tough time believing what we have accomplished. It is an accomplishment that I will cherish, not only for me, but also for my fa-, ther and all the people who have been the guideposts and mile markers down my own road—a road to the championship.[10]

⑤

STILL LEARNING

When Tony came to the NASCAR Cup circuit in 1999 he had already been racing for 20 years. It was quite an amazing accomplishment, considering he hadn't yet reached his 28th birthday. But even though Tony started racing at a very young age and had lots of experience as a professional driver, he still had a lot to learn about Cup racing. Unlike many other new Cup drivers, Tony had previously raced with the Indy Racing League (IRL) and had never raced in a Cup race before his rookie year.

"If you had the colors of the spectrum, Indy driving would be on one end and NASCAR would be on the other," explained Tony. "With an IRL car, you can go anywhere you want on the track. When you're driving a 3,400-pound stock car, you have to be more precise and find the [drive] line."

The first year of racing for any driver is a year of learning. Each time a driver gets into a different car or when his current car has been modified, he must master how to drive it so that he can take advantage of his assets. It is a learning experience for every driver, no matter how skilled he is. Being a rookie driver in a vehicle that is completely different from any vehicle you've ever driven means that there is a lot more learning to do. The other 1999 Nextel Cup rookies, Buckshot Jones and Elliott Sadler, both came from NASCAR's Busch

Tony Stewart sits inside the Home Depot No. 20 car and prepares to race in the Pennsylvania 500 at Pocono Raceway on August 1,2004. Tony has had his share of ups and downs during his career as an Indy and NASCAR driver.

Series. Both Jones and Sadler had competed in Nextel Cup races a few times during the 1998 season.

Tony knew that there would be a lot to master in his first year of Cup racing, so when he headed out on the Daytona International Speedway to qualify for the Daytona 500, mostly he was hoping that he wouldn't do anything to embarrass himself. Instead, Tony had the second-best qualifying time, meaning that he would start the race in second position. When a NASCAR Cup race starts, the cars are lined up in two rows around the track. The driver who qualifies first, in the pole position, is in the first car in line on the inside of the track, closest to the infield. A racer who qualifies second is in the "outside pole" position, or the first car in the line of drivers on the outside of the track.

"I've been preparing for this for 20 years," said Tony, "so even though it will be my first Winston Cup race, it's not as though I haven't been in this sort of position before. I started on the pole in my first Indianapolis 500, and I've been on the pole in a couple of Busch races."

After Tony had qualified on the outside pole for the Daytona 500, he competed in the Gatorade 125, a shorter event held at the Daytona International Speedway a few days before the big race. Because he knew he had already secured the second spot for the Daytona 500, Tony saw the Gatorade 125 as a race in which he wanted to learn as much as he could about the Daytona track.

During the 125-mile race, Tony tried lots of different driving techniques. He led for the first seven laps. Then Dale Earnhardt Sr., followed by a slew of other cars, came up behind him, trying to pass. To protect his lead, Tony drove forcefully to make sure that Earnhardt Sr. and the others would not get by. Eventually, however, Earnhardt Sr. passed Tony and went on to win. Within 10 laps, Tony had dropped from the lead to ninth position. By the end of the race, though, he climbed back toward the top, crossing the finish line in sixth place.

At the press conference after the race, Earnhardt Sr. told reporters what he thought of Tony's driving. "He's a mirror-driving son of a gun," said Earnhardt Sr., speaking of how Tony kept watching Earnhardt Sr. in his rearview mirror to make sure he could pass. "He's a good little racer, and he's got a good car. He'll learn. If it would have been the last lap of the Daytona 500, he'd have been spinning around into the grass," he said, indicating he would have bumped into Tony if the circumstances had been different.

In every race season, all drivers have their ups and downs. Tony has had his share of both during his time on the

NASCAR Cup circuit. During some of the down moments, he has let his temper get the best of him. In July of his rookie year, at the Jiffy Lube 300 in Loudon, New Hampshire, it looked as if Tony might get the first win of his NASCAR Cup career. Then, one of the worst things that can happen to a driver happened to Tony. With just two laps left in the race, he had to make a pit stop to get fuel, or he wouldn't have enough to finish the race. Tony gave up the lead, made a quick stop, and pulled back onto the track. He crossed the finish line in 10th place.

It was a disappointing moment, and Tony was angry. He had just lost his chance of winning because of a miscalculation that left him without enough gas to finish the race. When the race was over, he refused to talk to reporters. Later he explained,
"I always get in trouble when I lose, whether I blew an engine or got crashed or whatever, and that's when I stick my foot in my mouth. Then everybody seems to be like a vulture flying over my head."

It's true that some people criticized Tony, saying that he was immature and a bit arrogant. In some ways, this was true. Tony was, after all, one of the youngest drivers on the Cup circuit. He also came from the world of Indy car racing, where he had been a champion. But in Cup racing, he was the new kid on the block, trying to figure out exactly how everything worked, and it wasn't always easy.

The criticism sometimes made Tony defensive. He once told a reporter, "It gets disappointing because you have to mold yourself to what people want you to be. I am what I am, take me or leave me. If you don't like what you get, shop around the garage. There are 50 other guys [the other drivers], and you can find what you are looking for."

Even after five years in Cup racing, people were still criticizing Tony for his temper. In 2004, Tony had multiple incidents with his fellow drivers, both on and off the track. He used his race car to intentionally bump other drivers on the track and, after several races, he picked fights with fellow drivers. Tony's behavior left some drivers wondering about him. Driver Rusty Wallace said, "(Stewart) needs some help. He's in a ditch right now. I don't know what's wrong with the guy. He's really screwing up a lot lately."[11]

Although Tony sometimes lets his temper get the best of him, he also has some good friends among his fellow drivers and his crew. Tony and his crew chief, Greg "Zippy" Zipadelli, have been working together longer than any other driver-crew chief pair in the sport. Not only are they co-workers, they are friends. Tony said, "Relationships that you build in racing you never lose . . . . I don't think even if our

DID YOU KNOW?

The Victory Junction Gang Camp was founded by NASCAR driver Kyle Petty and his wife, Pattie, in honor of their son, Adam, who died in May 2000 during practice for a NASCAR Busch Series race in Louden, New Hampshire. The camp is located in Randleman, North Carolina, near the town of Greensboro. It is one of the camps in the Hole In The Wall Gang Camp system, which was founded by actor Paul Newman in 1986. Each Gang Camp has a theme, and Victory Junction's theme is racing. All of the buildings have a racing theme, including one that looks like a giant NASCAR race car. The camp is open to kids 7 to 15 years of age who have serious or life-threatening illnesses. The best part of all is that campers and their families get to visit Victory Junction for free.

Tony Stewart's crew chief and friend, Greg "Zippy" Zipadelli (center), sits on the pit box directing the crew and driver during a race. Tony believes that without Zipadelli, he could not have won the 2002 Nextel Cup championship.

future changes and we weren't with each other, I don't think the friendship would change."

Tony has also touched the lives of many through the Tony Stewart Foundation, a charity that he founded in 2003 to benefit multiple charities that help sick and disabled children. Tony's foundation contributes to many charities, including the Victory Junction Gang Camp, a camp for children with serious or life-threatening illnesses that was founded by NASCAR driver Kyle Petty and his wife Pattie. Shortly after starting his foundation, Tony promised to donate $1 million over a 10-year period to the Pettys' camp and said he hopes to be able to complete his donation in only five years.

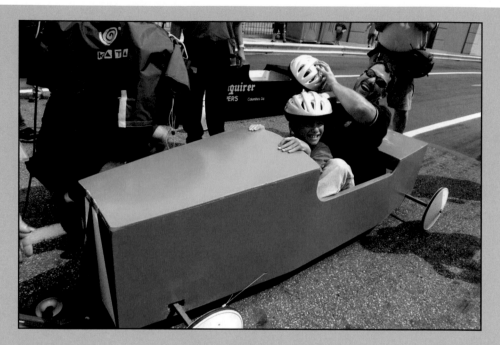

Tony Stewart, expert race car driver, still appreciates the thrill of competing in a soapbox derby. Racing is not only Tony's career; it's his hobby, too.

Knowing that his charity work is very different from the sometimes harsh personality he has on the track, Tony said, "What we do for a profession is one thing, but this is what you do for the kids. Every one of us in the garage area would do this, no matter what your image is or who you are."[12]

Racing is Tony's first love. The fact that he cares so much is one of the reasons he loses his temper. But it is also the reason why he is such a talented racer and why, when his peers are resting in their motor homes, he can often be found at a small dirt track racing with the local competition. Tony regularly competes in other types of racing during NASCAR's off-season, including the Chili Bowl and Turkey Night, two Midget races where the top racers compete against each other. In fact, Tony has expanded his interest in racing from driving to ownership. He owns a World of Outlaws team, five United States Auto Club teams, two three-quarter Midgets and one Legends car, and Eldora Speedway, a half-mile clay oval track in Rossburg, Ohio.

When Tony was in Talladega, Alabama, for the 1999 Nextel 500, he raced his late-model dirt-track car two nights before the Cup race. When Tony spoke about his three-day weekend of racing in Alabama, he enthusiastically talked about how busy he was going to be. He also acknowledged how different dirt-track racing was from Cup racing. "It should make for an interesting three days," he said. "It's like going from slipping and sliding down a country road to running wide open on Europe's Autobahn."

Tony put it best when he said, "I just love to race, no matter what type or where it's at . . . . Whether it's the Winston 500 or some little dirt-track race, I love it."

NOTES

Chapter 3

1. Joe Gibbs Racing, *Stewart snares sixth at Indy and third at Charlotte in Double Duty II*, JGR Press Release, May 28, 2001.

Chapter 4

2. Joe Gibbs Racing, *Stewart resilient following Daytona disappointment*, JGR Press Release, February 17, 2002.

3. Joe Gibbs Racing, *Stewart soldiers, but succumbs to Bristol*, JGR Press Release, March 24, 2002.

4. Joe Gibbs Racing, *Patience proves prosperous for Stewart at Richmond*, JGR Press Release, May 5, 2002.

5. Joe Gibbs Racing, *Stewart, Gibbs, Zipadelli and Home Depot comments regarding Brickyard 400 incident and subsequent resolutions*, JGR Press Release, August 8, 2002.

6. Tim Packman, *Troubles to triumph: Stewart wins at The Glen*, NASCAR.com, August 12, 2002. *www. nascar.com/2002/news/headlines/wc/08/11/watkins_ glen/*.

7. Tim Packman, *Win may be first difference for changed Stewart*, NASCAR.com, August 13, 2002. *www.nascar.com/2002/news/headlines/wc/08/12/ tstewart/*.

8.   Marty Smith, *Stewart is points leader for the first time in career*, NASCAR.com, October 7, 2002. *www.nascar.com/2002/news/headlines/wc/10/06/ tstewart_talladega/.*

9.   Ibid.

10.   Tony Stewart, "My Road to the NASCAR Winston Cup Championship," *Chicken Soup for the NASCAR Soul*, reprinted in NASCAR.com, April 8, 2003. *http://michael.froomkin.nascar.com/2003/news/head-lines/official/04/08/tstewart_chickensoup/.*

Chapter 5

11.   Marty Smith, *Stewart, Vickers involved in post-race incident*, NASCAR.com, June 28, 2004. *www.nascar. com/2004/news/headlines/cup/06/27/tstewart_ bvickers/.*

12.   Lee Montgomery, *Stewart to give Victory Junction Camp $1 million*, NASCAR.com, November 8, 2003. *http://icq.nascar.com/2003/news/headlines/ wc/11/08/tstewart_donation/.*

CHRONOLOGY

1971 Born on May 20 in Columbus, Indiana.

1979 Begins racing go-karts.

1983 Wins his first racing championship; named grand national champion by the International Karting Federation.

1989 Moves to Rushville, Indiana; begins racing three-quarter Midgets.

1991 Starts racing Sprint cars in addition to Midgets; is named United States Auto Club (USAC) Sprint Car Rookie of the Year.

1992 Begins racing Silver Crown cars in addition to Sprint cars and Midgets.

1995 Becomes the first and only driver to win the USAC "Triple Crown"—the Silver Crown, Sprint, and Midget championships—in the same year.

1996 Begins competing in the Indy Racing League (IRL) and is named Indy 500 Rookie of the Year; continues to race in the USAC league; starts to compete in NASCAR's Busch Grand National Series.

1997 Wins his first IRL race at Pikes Peak International Raceway in Colorado; wins the IRL championship.

1998 Competes in 22 NASCAR Busch Grand National races for Joe Gibbs Racing; continues racing full-time in IRL.

1999 Competes full-time in NASCAR Cup Circuit for Joe
Gibbs Racing; wins three races in his first Cup season, the most races ever won by a first-year driver;
is named Rookie of the Year; becomes first driver to
compete in and finish both the Indy 500 and Winston
Cup Coca-Cola 600 on the same day.

2000 Finishes in the top five at Rockingham, Las Vegas,
and Darlington; wins the Michigan 400.

2001 Competes in both the Indianapolis 500 and the Coca-
Cola 600 on the same day, placing sixth and third,
respectively.

Wins NASCAR Cup Championship.

2004 Wins Tropicana 400 and Sirius Satellite Radio At
The Glen.

STATISTICS

NASCAR Nextel Cup Series

Year	Races	Wins	Top 5	Top 10	Point Earnings	Standings
1999*	34	3	12	21	$3,190,149	4
2000	34	6	12	23	$3,642,348	6
2001	36	3	15	22	$4,941,463	2
2002	36	3	15	21	$9,163,761	1
2003	36	2	13	19	$6,136,633	7
2004	36	2	10	19	$6,221,710	6
*Rookie year						
Career	212	19	77	125	$33,296,064	

NASCAR Busch Series

Year	Races	Wins	Top 5	Top 10	Point Earnings	Standings
1996	9	0	0	0	$45,140	49
1997	5	0	1	2	$48,625	57
1998	22	0	5	5	$270,820	21
2003	1	0	0	0	$15,575	109
2004	4	0	2	2	$109,255	58
Career	41	0	8	9	$489,415	

(Note: Stewart did not compete in the NASCAR Busch Series in 1999 to 2002)

Indianapolis 500

Year	Start	Finish	Qualifying Speed	Laps Led	Earnings
1996	1	24	233.100	44	$222,053
1997	2	5	218.020	64	$345,050
1998	4	33	220.380	1	$220,250
1999	24	9	220.650	0	$186,670
2001	7	6	224.248	13	$218,850
Career	38	77		122	$1,192,873

(Note: Stewart did not compete in the Indianapolis 500 in 2000)

FURTHER READING

Canfield, Jack. *Chicken Soup for the NASCAR Soul.* Deerfield Beach, FL: HCI Publishing, 2003.

Close, John. *Tony Stewart: From Indy Phenom to NASCAR Superstar.* Osceola, WI: Motorbooks International, 2004.

Golenbock, Peter. *NASCAR Encyclopedia.* Osceola, WI: Motorbooks International, 2003.

Leebrick, Kristal. *Tony Stewart* (Edge Books: NASCAR Racing). Mankato, MN: Capstone Press, 2004.

Martin, Mark; Tuschak, Beth. *NASCAR for Dummies.* For Dummies, 2005.

Mitchell, Jason. *Tony Stewart: Driven to Win* (NASCAR Wonder Boy Collector's Series). Chicago, IL: Triumph Books, 2003.

Schaefer, A.R. *The History of NASCAR* (Edge Books: NASCAR Racing). Mankato, MN: Capstone Press, 2005.

Stewart, Tony; Bourcier, Mark. *True Speed: My Racing Life.* New York, NY: HarperEntertainment, 2002.

Other

Stewart, T., and Kid Rock. *NASCAR-Tony Stewart: Smoke*, DVD. Presented by NASCAR Images. Universal Music & VI, 2003.

Teitelbaum, Michael. *Tony Stewart: Instant Superstar* (World of NASCAR Series). Tradition Books, 2002.

Utter, Jim. *Tony Stewart: Hottest Thing on Wheels*. Sports Masters, 2000.

Woods, Bob. *NASCAR pit pass: behind the scenes of NASCAR* (NASCAR Middle Grade Book). Reader's Digest, 2005.

BIBLIOGRAPHY

Canfield, Jack. *Chicken Soup for the NASCAR Soul*. Deerfield Beach, FL: HCI Publishing, 2003.

Golenbock, Peter. *NASCAR Encyclopedia*. Osceola, WI: Motorbooks International, 2003.

Joe Gibbs Racing. *Patience proves prosperous for Stewart at Richmond*. JGR Press Release, May 5, 2002.

———. *Stewart, Gibbs, Zipadelli and Home Depot comments regarding Brickyard 400 incident and subsequent resolutions*. JGR Press Release, August 8, 2002.

———. *Stewart resilient following Daytona disappointment*, JGR Press Release, February 17, 2002.

———. *Stewart soldiers, but succumbs to Bristol*. JGR Press Release, March 24, 2002.

———. *Stewart snares sixth at Indy and third at Charlotte in Double Duty II*, JGR Press Release, May 28, 2001.

Martin, Mark and Beth Tuschak. *NASCAR for Dummies*. Hoboken, NJ: John Wiley & Sons, 2005.

Montgomery, Lee. *Stewart to give Victory Junction Camp $1 million*. NASCAR.com, November 8, 2003. *http:// icq.nascar.com/2003/news/headlines/wc/11/08/tstewart_donation/*.

Packman, Tim. *Troubles to triumph: Stewart wins at The Glen*. NASCAR.com, August 12, 2002. *www.nascar. com/2002/news/headlines/wc/08/11/watkins_glen/*.

———. *Win may be first difference for changed Stewart*. NASCAR.com, August 13, 2002. *www.nascar. com/2002/news/headlines/wc/08/12/tstewart/*.

Smith, Marty. *Stewart is points leader for the first time in career*. NASCAR.com, October 7, 2002. *www.nascar. com/2002/news/headlines/wc/10/06/tstewart_talladega/*.

———. *Stewart, Vickers involved in post-race incident*. NASCAR.com, June 28, 2004. *www.nascar.com/2004/ news/headlines/cup/06/27/tstewart_bvickers/*.

Stewart, Tony. "My Road to the NASCAR Winston Cup Championship." *Chicken Soup for the NASCAR Soul*, reprinted in NASCAR.com, April 8, 2003. *http:// michael.froomkin.nascar.com/2003/news/headlines/ official/04/08/tstewart_chickensoup/*.

Stewart, Tony and Mark Courcier. *True Speed: My Racing Life*. New York, NY: HarperEntertainment, 2002.

ADDRESSES

Indy Racing League
Indianapolis Motor Speedway
4790 West 16th Street
Indianapolis, IN 46222

Joe Gibbs Racing
13415 Reese Boulevard West
Huntersville, NC 28078

NASCAR
P.O. Box 2875
Daytona Beach, FL 32120
(386) 253-0611

Tony Stewart Fan Club & Tony Stewart Foundation
5644 West 74th Street
Indianapolis, IN 46278

INTERNET SITES

www.indycar.com

> *This website is the best place to start learning more about Indy car racing. It has the latest results and driver standings, but there are also pages where readers can learn more about the sport in general.*

www.joegibbsracing.com

> *Website for racing teams owned by Joe Gibbs.*

www.nascar.com

> *This website is the best place to start learning more about NASCAR. It has the latest results and driver standings, but there are also pages where readers can learn more about the sport in general.*

www.nascar.about.com

> *This website contains news about NASCAR racing and reviews of racers and races. It also provides open forums for discussion about various aspects of NASCAR.*

www.racingone.com

> *This website contains unfiltered NASCAR racing news about racers and races.*

www.tonystewart.com

> *The official Tony Stewart fan site.*

www.usacracing.com

This is the official USAC Racing website.

www.victoryjunction.org

This site provides information about the Victory Junction organization, the camp and the contributors, and links to news and ways to donate.

Photo Credits:

AP/Wide World Photos: Cover, 7, 12, 13, 16, 18, 20, 25, 33, 37, 40, 47. ©George Tiedemann/NewSport/CORBIS: 36, 43, 48. ©Getty Images: 9, 27, 28.

INDEX

ABOUT THE AUTHOR

Tara Baukus Mello is a freelance automotive writer. Since 1987, she has published more than 3,500 articles in newspapers and magazines and has authored 10 books. Baukus Mello is also the author of *Rusty Wallace*, *Mark Martin*, *The Pit Crew*, *The Need for Speed*, and *Stunt Driving*, all part of the RACE CAR LEGENDS series. A graduate of Harvard University, she lives in southern California, where she cruises the streets in her 1932 Ford pickup street rod with her husband, Jeff.